writing guides

ACTIVITIES FOR WRITING

Life STORIES

ANGEL SCOTT

NON-FICTION FOR AGES 9-11

CONTENTS

INTRODUCTION

The Scholastic *Writing Guides* series provides teachers with ideas and projects that promote a range of writing, bringing insights from educational research into the classroom. Each guide explores a different type of writing and provides example material, background information, photocopiable activities and teaching suggestions. Their aim is to enable teachers to guide the writing process, share planning ideas and develop themes as a context for writing activities.

The materials:

- motivate children with interesting activities
- break complex types of writing into manageable teaching units
- focus on and develop the typical features of particular types of writing
- provide original approaches to teaching.

Each book is divided into sections, beginning with examples of the type of writing being taught. These are followed by ideas for developing writing and projects that will extend over a series of sessions.

SECTION ONE: USING GOOD EXAMPLES

Section One looks at good examples of the genre, with the emphasis on using texts to stimulate and develop writing. Two example texts are shared, and questions that focus the discussion on their significant features are suggested. This is followed by activities that explore what the texts can teach us about writing, enabling teachers to compare the two texts and to go on to model the type of writing presented in the guide.

SECTION TWO: DEVELOPING WRITING

Section Two moves from reading to writing. This section provides activities that prompt and support children in planning and writing. A range of approaches includes planning templates and strategies to stimulate ideas. The activities refine children's ideas about the type of writing being developed and give them focused writing practice in the context of scaffolded tasks. Teacher's notes support each activity by explaining the objective and giving guidance on delivery.

SECTION THREE: WRITING

Section Three moves on to writing projects. Building upon the earlier work in Section Two, these projects aim to develop the quality of writing and provide a selection of ideas for class or group work on a particular theme or idea. The teacher may choose to use some or all of the ideas presented in each project as a way of weaving the strategies developed in Section Two into a more complex and extended writing task.

SECTION FOUR: REVIEW

Section Four supports the assessment process. Children are encouraged to reflect on the type of writing they are tackling and to evaluate how effectively their work has met the criteria for the genre identified in Section One.

Boy

The sweet-shop was the very centre of our lives. Without it, there would have been little to live for. But it had one terrible drawback, this sweet-shop. The woman who owned it was a horror. We hated her and we had good reason for doing so.

Her name was Mrs Pratchett. She was a small skinny old hag with a mouth as sour as a green gooseberry. She never smiled. She never welcomed us when we went in, and the only times she spoke were when she said things like, "I'm watchin' you, so keep yer thievin' fingers off them chocolates!" Or "I don't want you in 'ere just to look around! Either you *forks* out or you *gets* out!"

But by far the most loathsome thing about Mrs Pratchett was the filth that clung around her. Her apron was grey and greasy. Her blouse had bits of breakfast all over it, toast-crumbs and tea stains and splotches of dried egg-yolk. It was her hands, however, that disturbed us most. They were disgusting. They were black with dirt and grime. They looked as though they had been putting lumps of coal on the fire all day long. And do not forget please that it was these very hands and fingers that she plunged into the sweet-jars when we asked for a pennyworth of Treacle Toffee or Wine Gums or Nut Clusters or whatever. The mere sight of her grimy right hand with its black fingernails digging an ounce of Chocolate Fudge out of a jar would have caused a starving tramp to go running from the shop. But not us. Sweets were our life-blood. We would have put up with far worse than that to get them. So we simply stood and watched in sullen silence while this disgusting old woman stirred around inside the jars with her foul fingers.

from *Boy: Tales of Childhood* by Roald Dahl

Easter chicks

It was a tiny incident, something that's almost nothing, but it's stayed with me ever since it happened. It was mid-way through the school holidays, and I felt a great thrill of freedom as I walked out of the house alone, and out of the estate. I crossed Rectory Road, where the trees were in bright green leaf and grass was growing thickly on the verges, and entered the narrow lane to Windy Ridge, where the allotments were. The sun was shining. The greenhouses glittered. The air was filled with the scent of newly-turned earth and wood smoke.

I reached up and opened the gate. Grandad was sitting on the low brick wall of a cold frame. He wore his navy blue suit as always, his checked cloth cap as always, and was smoking his pipe as always. He turned to me as my feet crunched on the cinder path.

"Everybody all right?" he said.

"Aye."

"Howay, then. Something to show you."

Then he opened the door of the greenhouse: brilliant light and heat, and the sweet powdery scent of tomato plants. There was a cardboard box on a bench, a distant squeaking and scratching.

"Aye," he said. "In there."

I leaned closer and looked down into the box. There were a dozen chicks or more, tiny and bright yellow, shuffling together, squeaking together. I reached in and felt the sharp beaks and soft feathers, the delicate bodies trembling with new life. I lifted one from the box, cupped it in my hand, held it to my face. I laughed at the tiny claws scratching at my skin, at the tiny eyes, the tiny voice.

"Can this one be mine?"

"Aye. That one can be yours."

from *Counting Stars* by David Almond

A good autobiography is a selective account of things that the writer remembers, made interesting by the way they are described. It is a subjective account of experiences that left a lasting impression in the mind of the writer.

Shared activities

Explore the definition above with the children. Discuss the following features of life stories.

● *Subjectivity*: the writer gives us his or her personal response to things. The emotional content of autobiographies interests the reader – not only what happened but how the writer felt about it.

● *Objectivity*: there is a place for objective reporting about outside events. This reassures us that the autobiography is not a work of fiction.

● *Selectivity*: the writer chooses to recount only those events which have left a lasting impression.

● *Convincing description*: the writer uses evocative language and involves all of their senses to bring their experiences alive for the reader.

Boy extract

Read the extract on photocopiable page 4 from Roald Dahl's *Boy: Tales of Childhood* (Puffin) and focus on the description of the sweet-shop as *the very centre of our lives*. Look at the 'centres' of other people's lives, for example the football pitch, the mosque or the park. Ask the children why they think Mrs Pratchett said what she did. What might she say about the boys when they were not there? Do the children think Dahl has described the sweet-shop and its owner accurately? If not, why has he exaggerated? (To make the incident more interesting for the reader.)

Counting Stars extract

Read the extract on photocopiable page 5 from David Almond's *Counting Stars* (Hodder). The writer tells us that his story is not important, so why do we want to read on?

Point out how he tells us what he could see and feel and smell. Look closely at the description of the chicks; pinpoint the adjectives and verbs. How do the children think David is feeling? What makes them think that? Talk about how they gradually found out about the incident. Almond lets it unfold.

Look back at Grandad. What is he like? How do we know? Talk about the special role of grandparents (being sensitive about absent grandparents). Contrast Almond's grandad with Mrs Pratchett. What would Mrs Pratchett say about the chicks?

Mrs Pratchett

Distribute copies of photocopiable page 4. The autobiographical writer tries to describe events, people and places in a way that will make them interesting to the reader. Photocopiable page 8 focuses children's attention on this. They should find what Dahl says about Mrs Pratchett in the text, then write about how it makes them think and feel as a reader.

David's route

Distribute copies of photocopiable page 5. Another feature of autobiographical writing is that the writer evokes events and places by describing a variety of sense impressions. Photocopiable page 9 asks the children to follow David's journey from home to his grandad's greenhouse, noting what he saw, felt and so on at each step of the way.

Taking ideas further

So far, Section One has helped children to identify the important features of autobiographical writing. They are unlikely to have read very many examples of the genre and may think that only the life stories of extraordinary people will be worth reading. Reassure them that it is the way a life story is told that makes it interesting and that even the smallest incidents (as in 'Easter Chicks') can be fascinating to read. The extracts they have read have dealt with a grandad and the owner of a sweet-shop – characters that figure in many children's lives.

What do we know about the characters?

Photocopiable page 10 asks children to compare their impressions of these two characters. Tell them not to look back at the text but to write what they know about them from memory. When they have finished, discuss how vivid an image of each character we have. Help children to see that this is because we see each character through the eyes of someone who had very strong feelings about them. These portraits are not intended to be 'fair' or 'objective'.

Autobiography

Photocopiable page 11 is a genre map which can be used at the end of Section One to recap the significant features identified so far. Children can be asked to give an example of each point from the text extracts. It can also be enlarged and displayed as a prompt or a checklist for children working on Sections Two and Three, when they are writing or discussing their own autobiographies.

Mrs Pratchett

Look again at the text. Write what Roald Dahl says about Mrs Pratchett's words, her clothes and her hands. Then write what it makes you think and feel as a reader.

	What is said in the text	How it makes me think and feel as a reader
What Mrs Pratchett says		
What Mrs Pratchett is wearing		
Mrs Pratchett's hands		

David's route

Re-read 'Easter Chicks' and follow David's route on the map.
Write what David saw, felt and so on at each step.

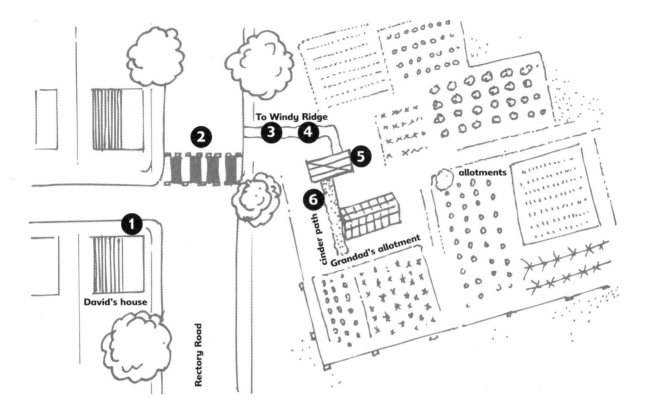

1 David felt _____

_____

2 He saw _____

_____

3 David saw _____

_____

4 He smelled _____

_____

5 He saw _____

_____

6 He heard _____

_____

What do we know about the characters?

Compare the two characters you have read about. Write what you know about them without referring back to the text.

	Mrs Pratchett	Grandad
What they look like		
What they do		
What they say		
What I think		

Autobiography
The story of your life

- Tell us what other people did and said.

- Write about the most important people and places in your life.

- Tell us what you saw heard touched smelled tasted.

- Write about key events in your life.

- Bring people and places alive, using vivid description.

- Tell us what you think feel believe.

- You are the main character. Write in the first person.

- Tell us what you said felt thought.

SECTION TWO

DEVELOPING WRITING

One of the common problems that children experience in writing is deciding what to write about. The joy of writing autobiography is that the material is already there. This frees the child to think more carefully about selection, structure and style. They can concentrate on using their imagination to bring their experience alive for the reader rather than inventing the incidents.

In Section One, the children read and discussed examples of autobiographical writing. They will be aware of the typical features of this type of writing and are ready to think about how they might tell the story of their own life.

The activities in this section will help them to identify the key events, people and places which will form the basis for their own autobiography. It is important that they consider what makes an autobiography interesting to read and to write.

Begin by reading the following quotation from Roald Dahl to the class.

'An autobiography is a book a person writes about his own life and it is usually full of all sorts of boring details…

I would never write a history of myself. On the other hand, throughout my young days at school and just afterwards a number of things happened to me that I have never forgotten.

None of these things is important, but each of them made such a tremendous impression on me that I have never been able to get them out of my mind. Each of them, after a lapse of fifty and sometimes sixty years, has remained seared on my memory.

I didn't have to search for any of them. All I had to do was skim them off the top of my consciousness and write them down.

Some are funny. Some are painful. Some are unpleasant. I suppose that is why I have always remembered them so vividly. All are true.'

What do the children think are the *boring details* that people don't want to read about? (Dates, facts, lists.) And what are the sort of things people *do* want to read about someone else's life? (The funny, scary, happy, sad times; the times that stand out; how the writer felt; what people said.) Tell the children that, in this section, they are going to collect material that could go into their own autobiography. Emphasise that you don't want them to write what Dahl calls a *history of myself* (lists of objective facts).

OTHER PEOPLE'S LIFE STORIES

WHAT YOU NEED

Examples of autobiographical writing (see page 23), display space.

WHAT TO DO

Talk about the different ways in which autobiographical material is presented – chronological accounts, letters, diaries, poems and so on. Show some examples and set up an autobiographical corner or display table. Point out that all these different types of writing share the important characteristic of autobiography: they bring alive incidents which, however apparently insignificant, made an impact on the writer.

Encourage the children to contribute examples from their own reading to the display. If they suggest books about someone else's life which have been written by another person (that is, not the person that the book is about), take the opportunity to reinforce the distinction between biography and autobiography.

OBJECTIVE
■ To become aware of different ways of presenting autobiographical material.

FACTFILE

WHAT YOU NEED

Materials to make a factfile, board or flip chart, writing materials.

WHAT TO DO

Discuss how facts give 'weight' to autobiographical writing. They put the personal incidents and experiences in context so that the reader knows that he or she is reading about events that actually happened. With the children, brainstorm some of the facts which they might want to include in their own autobiographies (when and where they were born; where they went to nursery or other school; where they have been on outings and holidays). They could also include staging points such as learning to walk, talk, ride a bike, swim and so on. Ask them how they would find out this information. Who would they ask? (Parents, grandparents, carers, teachers…)

Invite the children to start they own factfiles by making a list of the headings you have brainstormed, leaving space for the information to be filled in as they find it out. They can also include a column in which they write the sources of the information.

This activity can be ongoing alongside the rest of the work they are doing on autobiographical writing.

OBJECTIVES
■ To understand the need for facts and evidence to underpin autobiographical writing.
■ To understand that this information can come from a variety of sources.

THIS IS MY LIFE

WHAT YOU NEED

Photocopiable page 17, writing materials.

WHAT TO DO

Remind the children that a life story will only be as interesting as the events described in it. Invite them to think of special times in their lives and share them with the class. Can they remember saying or doing something funny or naughty when they were little? You may like to tell them about some of the moments from your own past which you remember vividly.

Ask the children to fill in copies of photocopiable page 17. They should write brief notes about their most special day, the funniest thing that happened to them, and so on. Tell them there is no need to complete the boxes in order. They can read through the headings and make notes about the things they remember best. If they

OBJECTIVE
■ To identify key events as a basis for telling one's life story.

are stuck on any boxes it may help if they talk in pairs about some of the things from their past.

As a separate activity, the blank photocopiable sheet can be enlarged, cut into separate boxes and given out to a group of nine children. Each child writes about a true story and the papers are shuffled and dealt out to the group. Children then guess who wrote the 'story' they were dealt.

Children can be invited to bring in items from home which record their special moments, such as postcards, certificates or photographs.

SIX YEARS

WHAT YOU NEED

Photocopiable page 18, board or flip chart, writing materials, scissors, paper, children's photographs from home (optional).

WHAT TO DO

Explain to the children that it is important to tell their life story in the order in which things happened. It is helpful to give the reader signposts by saying in which year things happened and to refer to other things that were going on at the time.

Look at the photographs together, if the children have brought some in from home. Ask individual children to offer significant memories. Explore when they occurred and write the year and the age of the child on the board as well as a note of the event described. Ask what else was happening in the child's life that year. What class were they in? Where were they living? Do they know of anything that was in the news that year? Make notes which will serve as a model for the activity.

Give the children copies of photocopiable page 18 and ask them to fill it in by making notes about the events of six different years in their lives. Maybe they will start with the year they learned to ride a bike, or moved house or the year their younger sibling was born. Remind them to think about the questions on the sheet. When they have filled in all six boxes they should cut them out and paste them down onto a separate sheet of paper in chronological order.

MOMENTS IN TIME

WHAT YOU NEED

Children's photographs from home (ideally each child should bring in three photographs from different years), board or flip chart, sugar paper for timeline, writing and drawing materials.

WHAT TO DO

As a class, discuss one or two of the children's photographs and make notes on the board. When was the photograph taken? What is happening in it? Who is shown in it? Where were they?

Now ask pairs of children to discuss the photographs they have brought in, using a similar 'When? What? Who? Where?' format. A wall display can be made in the form of a timeline, spanning the years of the children's lifetime. Photographs can be Blu-Tacked onto this, with indicator lines leading to the appropriate year. The child's name and brief details about where, who, and so on can be added next to the photo. If any children cannot bring in photographs, they could draw a photo-sized picture instead, to contribute to the timeline. Events they might focus on include: learning to walk or swim; getting or losing pets; moving house; starting or moving schools; journeys and holidays; celebrations such as birthdays, Eid, Diwali, Easter.

OBJECTIVE
■ To establish a chronology of events.

OBJECTIVES
■ To explore times in the past, using photographs as a starting point.
■ To create a class timeline.

INTERVIEW PLANNER

WHAT YOU NEED

Photocopiable page 19, writing materials.

WHAT TO DO

Talk with the children about what sources they could use for obtaining more information for their life stories. So far they have trawled their own memories and looked at photographs. They are likely to suggest their parents as sources; help them to see that there may be other people who have known them for a long time who may help them to fill out the picture of their lives, for example grandparents, uncles, aunts, neighbours, friends, staff at school. Different people will know about different aspects of their life: teaching assistants will remember things they did at school; grandparents may remember times when they were ill; neighbours may remember funny things they did or said. It is important to bear in mind, however, that when inviting children to explore their past in this way one must be sensitive to their home situations and family history.

Children should fill in each of the four boxes on photocopiable page 19 with the name of someone to interview and thoughts about a question they could ask that person. It may help them to work in pairs, discussing the sorts of things they might ask about. Children should be encouraged to carry out interviews with their named people and to make further notes on a separate sheet. These notes can later be incorporated into their autobiography.

OBJECTIVE
■ To provide children with a framework for interviewing adults who knew them when they were younger.

PLACES IN MY LIFE

WHAT YOU NEED

Photocopiable page 20, writing materials.

WHAT TO DO

Explore with the children what makes a place memorable. Emphasise that the place may not be obviously special to other people but that it can be memorable because of what happened to you there or how you felt when you went there. It might be a corner of your back garden or it might be a place you have only visited once.

Look again at the text on page 5 and discuss what was memorable about the allotments for the young David Almond. Draw attention to the fact that the writer mentions not only sights and sounds but also smells.

Ask the children to complete photocopiable page 20 by thinking of three places that are memorable for them. They should make notes about why each place is memorable and note the things they remember seeing, hearing and smelling there. As preparation for this, invite them to shut their eyes, conjure up the place in their imagination and ask themselves what they can see/hear/smell/feel/taste. They may like to draw a picture of one of their memorable places to be used to illustrate the autobiography they will be writing later.

As an extra activity, ask the children to write a paragraph which describes one of their places. They should describe the setting in a way which evokes what was special about it, including sounds, sights and smells.

OBJECTIVES
■ To identify places that have been important or which are memorable.
■ To draw on a variety of senses when describing a setting.

OBJECTIVE

■ To focus on people who have been significant in the children's lives.

PEOPLE IN MY STORY
WHAT YOU NEED
Photocopiable page 21, writing materials, children's photographs from home (optional).

WHAT TO DO
Talk with the children about the people who have had an impact on their lives. Encourage them to think beyond immediate family, for example people at school (a dinner helper or a crossing patrol); people they see at weekends (someone who runs a football game or a neighbour who always smiles). Encourage them to look back and to think also about 'memorable' people in the same way as they thought about memorable places (someone whom they may only have seen once but who they remember for some reason). It may be a person who visited school a long time ago; someone from playgroup or whom they met on holiday. Once again, children may be able to bring in photographs to support this activity.

Ask the children to fill in photocopiable page 21. The first three boxes invite them to think of people in specific categories but they are free to suggest the reason why they have chosen the last person. Many children will have more special people that they want to write about and they should be encouraged to make notes on two or three more people on a separate sheet.

You may also like to ask them to write a paragraph about one of their special people. Remind them how Roald Dahl depicted Mrs Pratchett and that he almost certainly exaggerated her characteristics. Tell them they should try to bring their person to life by focusing on the details that make him or her special and exaggerating them to bring them alive for the reader.

OBJECTIVES

■ To record a memorable conversation.
■ To focus on the way people speak.

WHAT PEOPLE SAID
WHAT YOU NEED
Photocopiable page 22, board or flip chart, writing materials.

WHAT TO DO
Tell the children that you want them to think about a conversation that was important to them. It might have happened recently or when they were little. Reassure them that it is not easy to remember exactly what people say, but as long as they can remember what the conversation was about and the way each person spoke, they can 'fill it out' to make a convincing dialogue.

Demonstrate this, in a shared session, by inviting a child to tell the class about a memorable conversation. It may have been when someone was specially pleased or angry with them. Maybe they had hurt themselves and someone was kind. Perhaps they had lost something (or were themselves lost) and someone was helpful. Can they remember anything that they or the other person said? Jot it down. If not, ask the child to try to think themselves back into the situation. How did each person feel? What do they *think* each person said? Make some notes on the board.

Then, together, write what one of the people said. You may have to invent the actual words, but emphasise how important it is to try to keep with the real mood or feeling of the situation and the personalities involved. How old was each person? How would they have spoken? Did the other person use lots of words or a few? Did they use slang or not?

When you have written several lines of dialogue in this way, give the children copies of photocopiable page 22 and ask them to write their own conversation. It should arise from a real event in their past and be based on a conversation which really took place.

This is my life

Think of important things in your life. Write about your…

oldest memory	most special day	most important visit
most scary experience	**biggest argument**	**good friend**
funniest time	**important object**	**special place**

Make brief notes about each of these.

Six years

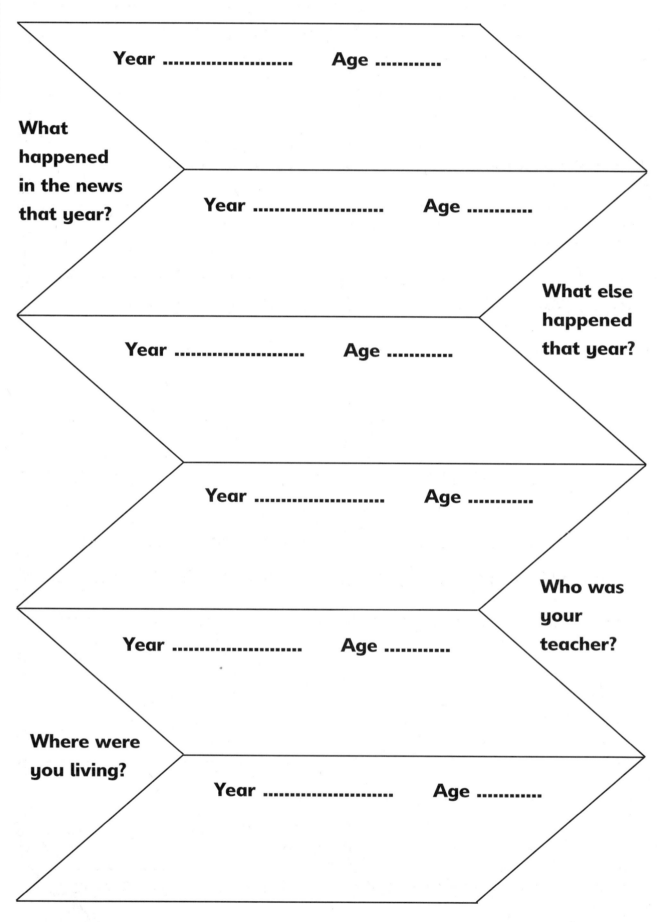

Year .... Age ....

What happened in the news that year?

Year .... Age ....

What else happened that year?

Year .... Age ....

Year .... Age ....

Who was your teacher?

Year .... Age ....

Where were you living?

Year .... Age ....

writing guides: **LIFE STORIES**

Interview planner

Plan interviews with four people who knew you when you were little.
They could be family, friends or neighbours of staff
at school, for example.

Interviewee _____

I could ask about _____

_____

_____

_____

One question to ask:

_____

_____

_____

Interviewee _____

I could ask about _____

_____

_____

_____

One question to ask:

_____

_____

_____

Interviewee _____

I could ask about _____

_____

_____

_____

One question to ask:

_____

_____

_____

Interviewee _____

I could ask about _____

_____

_____

_____

One question to ask:

_____

_____

_____

Places in my life

Think of three places that have been important in your life.
What made them special?

Place _____

Why it is memorable _____

_____

| Things to see | Sounds and smells |

Place _____

Why it is memorable _____

_____

| Things to see | Sounds and smells |

Place _____

Why it is memorable _____

_____

| Things to see | Sounds and smells |

writing guides: **LIFE STORIES**

People in my story

Think of people who will feature in your life story.
Make notes for a story about them.

Someone who cares for me

Name

_ _ _ _ _ _ _ _ _ _ _ _

_ _ _ _ _ _ _ _ _ _ _ _

Story idea

_ _ _ _ _ _ _ _ _ _ _ _

_ _ _ _ _ _ _ _ _ _ _ _

_ _ _ _ _ _ _ _ _ _ _ _

_ _ _ _ _ _ _ _ _ _ _ _

Someone who gives good advice

Name

_ _ _ _ _ _ _ _ _ _ _ _

_ _ _ _ _ _ _ _ _ _ _ _

Story idea

_ _ _ _ _ _ _ _ _ _ _ _

_ _ _ _ _ _ _ _ _ _ _ _

_ _ _ _ _ _ _ _ _ _ _ _

Someone who makes me laugh

Name

_ _ _ _ _ _ _ _ _ _ _ _

_ _ _ _ _ _ _ _ _ _ _ _

Story idea

_ _ _ _ _ _ _ _ _ _ _ _

_ _ _ _ _ _ _ _ _ _ _ _

_ _ _ _ _ _ _ _ _ _ _ _

Someone who _ _ _ _ _ _ _

_ _ _ _ _ _ _ _ _ _ _ _

Name

_ _ _ _ _ _ _ _ _ _ _ _

_ _ _ _ _ _ _ _ _ _ _ _

Story idea

_ _ _ _ _ _ _ _ _ _ _ _

_ _ _ _ _ _ _ _ _ _ _ _

_ _ _ _ _ _ _ _ _ _ _ _

What people said

Think of a time when a person said something to you that you have remembered. In the speech bubbles, write what you said and what the other person said, to make a conversation.

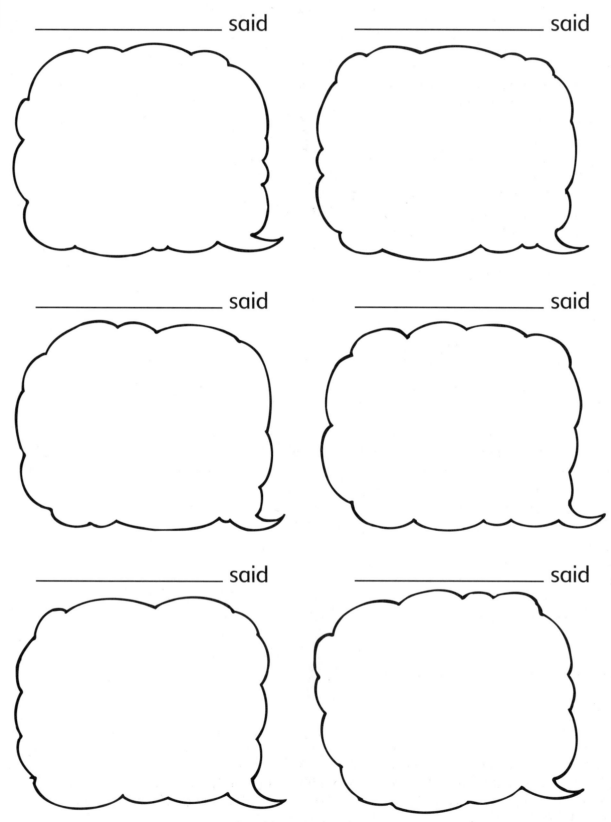

_____ said

_____ said

_____ said

_____ said

_____ said

_____ said

writing guides: LIFE STORIES

This section helps the children to develop an extended piece of writing, drawing on the ideas they have explored in the previous two sections. The activities support children in planning and writing a 'mini book' with chapters that tell their life story. This can be organised chronologically or thematically. For example, they can base their book on chronologically ordered key events, devoting each chapter to one of them. Alternatively, they can choose a number of important people and places, and base a chapter on each of these. In either case they can add a concluding chapter in which they reflect on their life so far and on what is important to them.

It will be helpful for children to have access to the photocopiable sheets they completed in Section Two together with their interview notes (page 19) and any photographs they may have brought in. They can also incorporate selected facts from their factfiles (page 13), but warn them against using too many or allowing them to take the form of a list. While being encouraged to refer back to these resources, they should also be free to conduct further interviews or seek more information and photographs from home, if necessary.

To help them with their own writing, give the children the opportunity to browse and read the work of other writers of life stories. Some that you may like to introduce into the classroom are:

- **Coming to England** *by Floella Benjamin (Puffin)*
- **Out of India** *by Jamila Gavin (Pavilion Books)*
- **Memories: an Autobiography** *by Mem Fox (Heinemann)*
- **War Boy** *by Michael Foreman (Puffin)*
- **After the War Was Over** *by Michael Foreman (Puffin)*
- **The Diary of a Young Girl** *by Anne Frank (Puffin)*
- **Zlata's Diary** *by Zlata Filipovic (Puffin)*

Poets like Michael Rosen and Jackie Kay also write poems about their lives, to which the children could refer.

The times of my life

Children will now have a lot of material they can draw on and will need to select the 'best' bits before deciding how to organise it. First they should gather together the work they did in Section Two and choose the most memorable events or 'people and places' in their lives so far. They can then select the six most important and be offered the choice of organising their life stories as a series of events in chronological order or as a non-chronological collection of chapters, each dealing with a person or a place.

Whichever they choose, tell them that each of their selected 'stories' will be the subject of one chapter in their autobiography, so they must be sure that each will be interesting to their readers. To focus their attention on this, tell them to make detailed notes on photocopiable page 25 on *how* they will make it interesting for a reader. Encourage them to think about what aspects of the event or the person they will emphasise (*I will make sure that the event is very funny; I will make the place seem very comfortable or scary; I will emphasise how old or helpful the person was,* and so on).

Planning my life story

Tell the children that they are going to write a plan of their life story in seven chapters. Using the work they did on photocopiable page 25, they should think of a title for each chapter. Tell them that the last chapter will sum up their life so far. They also need a title for their book, but this can be decided later. The completed photocopiable sheet will be a 'contents' list, which they can use as a book plan on which to jot down notes during the writing process. (This could be made easier if the sheet is stuck onto a larger blank sheet of paper.)

The Detail: YOU

Photocopiable page 27 encourages the children to explore their experiences in detail. Explain that each time they are going to write a chapter they can use this sheet to make notes. They are also asked to reflect on what they thought and felt in retrospect.

They are asked what they wish they had said. Talk about how we often don't say what we would like to. Or we think later of clever, funny or sharp things we might have said. Ask the children to think of the things they might have said as well as the things they did say. Suggest that they try to identify the 'mood' of the event – was it funny, sad or exciting, for example? Explain that they may exaggerate the mood of the time or place to give a strong 'flavour' and bring it alive for the reader.

Partner writing

Photocopiable page 28 is a paired planning activity. It can be used either when the children are working on the above activities or at a later stage in writing their life story. They should cut out the questions on the sheet and, when they have a scene to write, they can use them as a basis for quizzing each other about the event in question. The notes they make as they are answering can later be fed into their writing plan.

The last chapter

The last chapter of the autobiography can be used by the children to look back over their lives so far: to sum up who they are now, having experienced all the events, people and places which have been described in the earlier part of their autobiography. Tell them not to rush to write the first thing they think of in response to the prompts on photocopiable page 29. Encourage them to think quietly for a few minutes and reflect on all the experiences they have had.

For lower-ability children, the completed photocopiable sheet can be used as their final chapter. Higher-ability children can make notes which they elaborate into a fuller, more developed chapter.

The times of my life

Choose the six most memorable events or people and places in your life so far.

Events or 'people and places'

How I will make it interesting to a reader

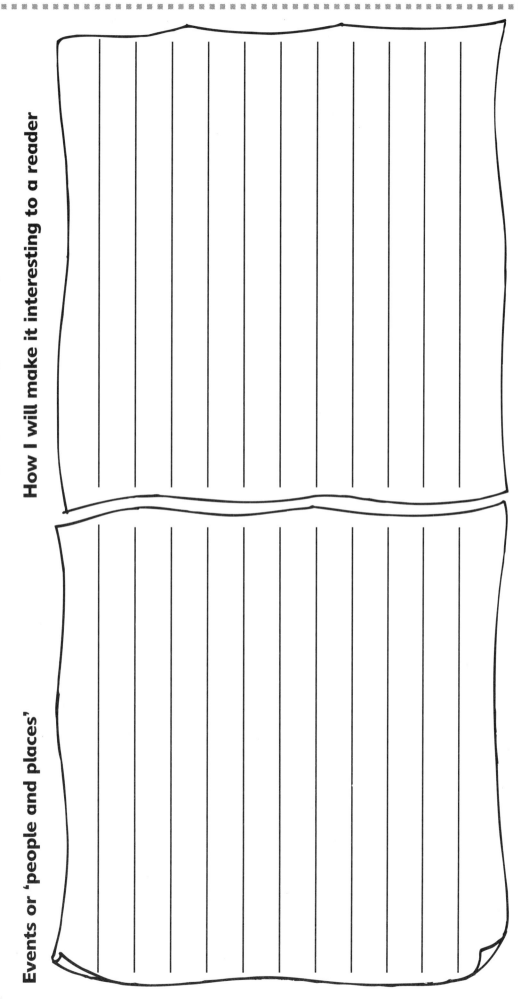

Number them in the order in which you will put them in your life story.

Planning my life story

How my autobiography is organised:

- key events in chronological order ☐

- people and places. ☐

Think of a title: _____

Write chapter titles. *Chapter 7 should sum up and look back.*

Chapter 1 _____

Chapter 2 _____

Chapter 3 _____

Chapter 4 _____

Chapter 5 _____

Chapter 6 _____

Chapter 7 _____

The detail: YOU

When you are writing a chapter, make detailed notes about your thoughts and feelings first.

Main event: _____

When was it? _____

Where was it? _____

I said _____

_____

I _wish_ I had said _____

_____

I thought _____

_____

I felt _____

_____

Afterwards, I felt _____

_____

Looking back on it I now, I think _____

_____

I will always remember _____

_____

because _____

_____

Partner writing

Cut out the questions. When you have a scene to write, use them with a partner to explore the details.

Think of 3 things that happened during this event.

_____

_____

_____

Describe the place where this event took place.

_____

_____

_____

What were you thinking at this time?

_____

_____

_____

What happened after this event?

_____

_____

_____

Think of a conversation that took place. What did people say?

_____

_____

_____

How did you feel at that time?

_____

_____

_____

What expressions were on people's faces?

_____

_____

_____

Why was this a special time?

_____

_____

_____

The last chapter

Look back over your life so far. Think carefully and complete these
sentences. Use your ideas to help you write your final chapter.

Title _____

_____

_____

In my life so far _____

_____

_____

The places which are most important are:

_____

_____

_____

The people who are most important are:

_____

_____

_____

What I dislike most is _____

_____

What I love most is _____

_____

I am glad I _____

_____

In the future I hope _____

_____

SECTION FOUR
REVIEW

This section helps children to identify the strengths and weaknesses of their life stories writing and encourages them to read others' work critically. It provides opportunities for you to review how well the children have understood what is required when writing autobiography.

Remind the children of the typical features of autobiographical writing (referring to page 11), when they are reviewing their work. Encourage them also to look back at the work done in Section Two.

It was funny because…

Photocopiable page 31 encourages the children to pick out the parts of their life stories that had a particular effect. This will enable them to identify the parts that worked well and should help them when it comes to revising their work. If they seek ways to emphasise the effect they have identified, it will make each chapter distinctive and make their writing more powerful.

They can go on to consider the adjectives which they have not selected. In conversation with their writing partner, this might stimulate them to think of things they have left out of their life stories.

I like that bit!

Photocopiable page 32 enables children to act as helpful writing partners, giving constructive feedback. They can read work in progress and use the sheet to help their partner revise their work and produce an improved final version. When evaluating their finished work, you may also like to use photocopiable page 32 yourself, as well as taking into account the work children did in Section Two. This will give you an idea of how well they handled the features of autobiography when they were focusing on the structured tasks.

It was funny because…

Look at your life story and find three events. Each must match one of the descriptive words on the right. Write the adjective and what the event was. Then say why you used that adjective to describe it.

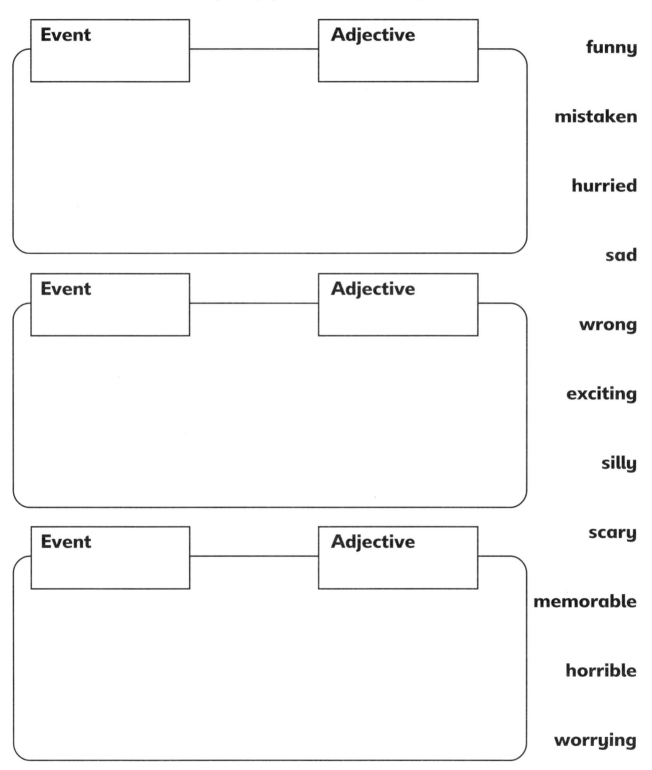

Event		Adjective

funny

mistaken

hurried

sad

wrong

exciting

silly

scary

memorable

horrible

worrying

Can you revise your work to make the event seem more horrible/ worrying/happy, and so on?

I like that bit!

Read your partner's life story. Help them to make their work better by filling in these boxes.

I enjoyed reading this life story

because _____

_____

_____

_____

My favourite part was

_____

_____

because _____

_____

_____

The description of _____

_____ **(a person)**

was great. It could be even better

if _____

_____

_____

I liked the conversation between

_____ **and**

_____ **.**

It might be even better if

_____

_____

_____

The description of _____

_____ **(a place)**

was really good. It could be even

better if _____

_____

_____

The most important event seemed

to be _____

_____

It could be funnier/sadder/more interesting/exciting/scary if

_____

_____

_____

I would have liked to know more about

_____

_____

_____

_____

writing guides: **LIFE STORIES**